DOWN FOR THE COUNT

Bouncing Back from Life's Blows

Compiled by Felicia C. Lucas
Volume IV

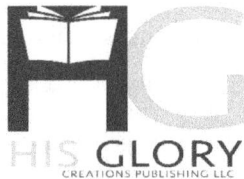

His Glory Creations Publishing, LLC
Wendell, North Carolina

This book is dedicated to individuals who are facing impossible situations and are seeking some inspiration in order to make it through the storm.

CONTENTS

Acknowledgements

Author Dr. Michelle Lucas

First and foremost, I would like to thank God who is the center of my life. I could not have made it without Him. I thank my parents Curtis Lucas who was a visionary and my mother, Jerolean Swann Lucas who pushed me to be all I could be and taught me to never give up. "The Village," the Swann and Lucas families who served as positive influences throughout my life. My church family, friends and colleagues, that held my hand during my journey. I would like to thank Minister Felicia Lucas for giving me to opportunity to express myself through writing. Lastly, I would like to thank my son, Millen, who is my best friend for life.

Author Tanya DuBose-Smith

Thank you to my family, the father of my son, my friend Rochelle F. Williams, and every person that stood by my side during one of the darkest periods of my life. Thank you to Minister Felicia Lucas for providing the opportunity to share how something so painful led me to growing into the person I am and embracing new heights of compassion for others. Thank you to Ms. Kim Roderick for all your encouragement, and prayers, and for being obedient to the leading of God. This was my set time to share this part of my life. Thank you to each person that invests in the purchase of this book. My hope is that some part of my journey will help you.

Author Stephanie Debman

I would like to first and foremost give thanks to my Lord and Savior Jesus Christ. I would also like to give a special thanks of gratitude to my husband as well as my children for helping me grow into the person that I am today. I thank Minister Felicia Lucas for giving me the golden opportunity to do this wonderful project, Down for the Count, which has helped me in doing a lot of research. I came to know about so many new things. I am thankful to her.

Secondly, I would also like to thank my Aunt and my siblings for always being by my side through thick and thin. No matter what, they loved me through it all. I dedicate this to my sister Keisha Spellman. May she rest in paradise! I know she is proud of her little sister.

Author Stephanie V. Barnes

Thank you God, for giving me the wisdom and ability to present my story to the world. A special thanks to my wonderful parents (Sammie Barnes and Bessie/Kenneth Lynch) and my incredible siblings (Deborah/Reginald Rawls and Kevin Barnes) who have loved me through many "chapters" of life. To my extended family (aunts, uncles, cousins), friends and ministry family, you all played an integral role in laying a strong foundation on which I am standing! To my spiritual coach (Dr. Edwards), I appreciate you believing in me and allowing me to grow under your leadership! Finally, I am thankful for the gift of our compiler, Minister Felicia Lucas and the publishing team. I'm honored to be a part of a project that is transforming lives!

AUTHOR ANTOINETTE BEY

I thank God for creating & keeping Antoinette Jeffries! Thank you Mama for your errors. Without them I wouldn't be who I am today! Thank you to my daughters, TeLeah for your insight and Danyiel for reminding me that I can never give up. My sons, Drace for adding depth to my understanding in ways he doesn't understand himself, JaMarae for reminding me to "Keep ya head up and Stay Motivated." Thank you, Shay Annette for being an awesome example to follow & always having a post-it available (insider). Thank you, Carolyn Ulrich, for reminding me that I do deserve God's best. Thank you, Quentin Bey, for your selfless love towards us. You are the BEST and I love you always (Kiss, Kiss)!

AUTHOR CALOTTA DAVIS

Giving God the praise for the opportunity to write my chapter in Down for The Count, Volume IV. Always honoring my Pastor and husband Samuel Davis for his never-ending support. To my family and friends for their love and support for encouraging me to write. God has strategically placed His greatness in me and through my obedience to carry out His will for my life; here I am today, a Co- Author. As I build the Kingdom of God, I interview authors and recording artist and business owners. I am following my dream to become an Author and pursuing my destiny. I dedicate this book to my Divine Women "Ministering to The Scars of a Woman" and now my scars are healed.

Author Clara Darden Pitt

I thank Almighty God for choosing, gracing and strengthening me to experience His love and power. I thank my husband, Dennis Pitt, for all his love and support. I thank my deceased mother, Ella Mae, for showing me how to endure. Thank you to my son, Alfred Theron, for reminding me of my strengths. Thanks to my dad, Clarence, and my siblings, Ella, Lisa and Marcus for loving me more in my days of weakness. Thanks to my grandmother, Jannie, my pastor: Apostle Edwards/Lady Edwards and others for their prayers and encouragement. Thanks to Minister Felicia Lucas for the opportunity to share this part of my story. I give all glory, honor and praise to my Lord and Savior, Jesus Christ, for His faithfulness.

Author Perita H. Adams

First of all, I would be remised if I didn't give Glory and Honor to God from whom all blessings flow. My gifts and talents to write my portion of this book comes from God himself. I pray that all who read it will always fight and never give up. I would also like to thank my family for all their love and support in the process. You inspire and motivate me to be a vessel for so many others who fight daily through depression, abuse-physical and mental, cancer and other health concerns. Louis and Antonio, you guys rock!! Special thanks to my friends: Wilhemenia FluEllen, Jennifer Corbett, Elizabeth Risher, Doretta Hightower, and so many more who have always stood by me in the process. Lastly, but not least, thanks to my church family at Joy Church, Sharon Forrest Baptist, and Central Church of God for all their love, guidance, and leadership. Thanks to Tyler Perry, Joel Osteen and Pastor John Gray for words of encouragement and inspiration in your messages. Keep it up! Believe me. You are reaching more people than you know.

COMPILER FELICIA C. LUCAS

Thank you God for this opportunity to connect these wonderful individuals during this portion of their journey. To my husband, friend and business partner Kelvin, thank you for your support! I love you!!! To my children, family, clients and friends who have supported me on my literary journey, I appreciate each of you! To my His Glory Creations Publishing LLC team, thank you for everything! You Rock!

FOREWORD

Oftentimes in life we are confronted with visible obstacles that seem to hinder our forward progress. However, over the course of time we manage to press our way through them. But what about the invisible obstacles? The greatest obstacles we typically face in life are not visible, but rather invisible. The Apostle Paul writes in Ephesians 6:12, "We wrestle not against flesh and blood, but against.......spiritual....." He emphasizes the internal of the struggle, which is invisible to us. But highly visible to God!

The truth of the matter is that you sometimes find yourself down, because of the imagination and thought process of the mind. Now it can be your mind, someone else's mind or a combination of the two that contribute to your degeneracy. For example, if you like watching the debilitating action of pornography, you have made up in your mind to watch something debilitating that originated in the mind of someone else. TOGETHER, you have created an invisible collaboration in the mind to watch what they produced. It's called MIND GAMES, and every time you engage yourself in a debilitating action, whether it be; smoking, drinking, and the like, you are losing the game!

However, the key to winning is to tap into the one who specializes in the invisible. Check out 2 Corinthians 10:4-5 which reads, "For the weapons of our warfare are not carnal, but mighty through God to the pulling down of strong holds; Casting down

imaginations and every high thing that exalteth itself against the knowledge of God, and bringing into captivity every **thought** to the obedience of Christ."

In other words, make a decision to:

1. GET UP
2. Grab the mighty weapons in Ephesians 6:14 (Truth & Righteousness), 15 (The Gospel), 16 (Faith), 17 (Salvation & The Word of God) along with 18 (Prayer)
3. Go to work with your arsenal of invisible spiritual weapons and start pulling this crazy stuff down in your life. You bring it down into captivity, rather than letting it bring you down!

WHAT ARE YOU WAITING FOR? LET'S GO!

Pastor Kelvin K. Lucas
Director/Founder of Take It By Force Ministries, Inc.
www.simplykelvin.com

Introduction

Have you ever watched a boxing match? There are two individuals in the boxing ring who desire to win each round. The first few rounds normally go smooth. Each of the boxers are getting in a few punches to their opponent. As each round gets higher and higher, they begin to move slower and depending upon their level of tolerance of pain; they continue to fight back or endure the punches from their opponent.

Have you ever gone through something in life which shook the very core of your existence? Have you ever lost something or someone who was very close to you? Have you experienced a treacherous situation and you had no clue if and when you would make it through? Have you felt the blows of life which can cause an individual to fall down and be in a very dark and lonely stage in life?

Just as a boxer experiences those blows that cause them to fall to their knees, we sometimes go through situations that seem impossible for us to rise above. Down for the Count occurs when one of the opponents are knocked down in the ring, and they are unable to rise within ten seconds. This boxer who has been knocked down will lose the fight if they cannot get up before the referee counts to ten. 10-9-8-7-6.... GET UP....5-4-3-2, as the crowd begins to cheer...1—then the bell sounds to end the round.

This book speaks to the individual who is down, in a low place in life and they struggle to get back on their feet again. Just like in a boxing match, you can be making your way back up and then you may not have the strength to rise again. Generally, when this happens, the boxer's coach and the crowd begin to cheer and shout to encourage the boxer to keep moving.

The co-authors in this book share their stories of how they experienced some adverse situations and how they ultimately bounced back from it. My desire is as you read the stories, you are inspired and encouraged to hang on. We want you to know that out there in this world there is someone who has a similar experience and ultimately bounced back!

By: Felicia C. Lucas

Chapter 1
Birthing my Purpose

By: Tanya DuBose-Smith

"My grace is sufficient for you, for my power is made perfect in weakness." –2 Corinthians 12:9

There have been numerous valley and mountaintop experiences that I have experienced through the grace of God keeping me. The day that I found myself in my doctor's office being informed I was pregnant with my first child was interesting. It was truly a day of joy, fear, and a cloud of questions that I flung at my doctor. Sitting on the examination table arguing back and forth with my doctor demanding he prove my pregnancy was real. You would have to truly understand the dialogue that my doctor and I normally had. Due to me being so adamant that I was not pregnant, he gave me an ultrasound. Hearing the heartbeat of the child I carried, the reality of it all began to sink in. This moment was truly one of a few that brought me pure joy, reacquainted my smile back to my face, and ceased the tears that had fallen so frequently since the transition of my maternal grandmother months earlier.

As I began to grow more comfortable with my new reality, I realized it would soon be time to share my news with those close to me and I was not sure of how each person would receive the news I was so elated about. In sharing the arrival of a new family member with my child's father it was honestly one of a very few times that I experienced him being completely speechless. Once the initial shock wore off my child's father and I spoke of how we felt about the news. He listened attentively as I shared that my dream of my own family had become a reality. That all the steps I had taken since 15 years old preparing for college was set in motion to one day be able to sustain myself and my own family.

In sharing the news with my family to say they were not happy was an understatement. During the time I was informed of my pregnancy, I was unemployed and due to a life-threatening illness years earlier, I had limited usage of my left arm. I was asked why I allowed myself to get pregnant in my later years, what I intended to do, and strong urges to end my pregnancy were made. I experienced a sea of voices that had constantly encouraged me to always go after my dreams that were now telling me how incapable I was of being a mother. This for me made me extremely sad and filled me with an anger I found difficult to express. The feelings of fear, loneliness, resentment, and eventually bitterness seasoned my interactions with family members I once treasured above all else. The questions of how in one breath, the words I love you flowed so easily, yet other seeds of doubt were frequently sown. To add insult to injury, an aunt I thought highly of told my mother that when she learned of my pregnancy, she immediately knew that my mother would be completely responsible for my unborn child.

As the months seem to speed by, I began to hear the opinions of those that meant well, overshadowing my own voice. I lost my confidence and began to purposely sleep to avoid questions or comments made regarding mine and my child's future. It felt like the only people that were happy yet nervous about the arrival of my child was the father and me. The father of my child was the only person that constantly spoke to me of my capacity to be a great mother and encouraged me by reminding me of the infant I had taken care of. The months that followed were not easy, as on one side my family not happy with my decision; on the other side was the father of my child and I encouraging each other while trying to embrace pockets of happiness over the pending arrival of our child. As I neared the timeframe where the termination of my pregnancy would be viable, a doctor's appointment was made. I was told that my presence was mandatory. On the day of my appointment my family and I minus my child's father arrived in separate cars. During the appointment with my doctor, myself, and my mother, I was provided with all the information on why I should not carry my child to term. I was strongly urged to terminate my pregnancy and I refused to comply with what was being suggested. It was at this point, I collected myself and my items leaving my mother there for my brother to pick her up.

Once I reached my seventh month my doctor scheduled me for a targeted ultrasound to ensure my baby was progressing normally. It was during this appointment that the ground once again shifted under my feet completely knocking me for a loop. After what felt like an eternity of nurses and techs shuffling in and out of the room speaking in hushed tones around myself and my mother, I was greeted by a doctor, a nurse, and tech that explained that my baby would not survive. My child whose sex had not been determined, would be born stillborn or die shortly after birth. I was sitting in the office with a genetics social worker that attempted to take her time answering my questions and providing me with tons of information on my child's diagnosis of Meckel-Gruber Syndrome.

It was time to take the ride back home to discuss what I learned with the father of my child who had to work and could not attend the appointment. Upon arriving home, I spoke with my child's father and his response broke my heart. I could hear the hurt in his voice. He asked me several of the same questions that I had asked just hours earlier.

The following week was filled with me bargaining with God, asking him questions, being filled with anger, rage, and sadness. Never having experienced labor pains, I mistook my contractions for being constipated and spent most of the day going from my bedroom to the bathroom, because oddly enough sitting on the toilet brought me relief. The next hours were spent between two different hospitals and attempts to stop my labor. After being told that my contractions were stopped, I was released and sent home. As I was being wheeled out to my mother's car, I continued to tell the nurses that I'm still in pain and that my contractions had not stopped.

Only to take an hour nap and awaken to more intense labor pains, I was once again back in between the restroom and my bedroom. Until I could not bear the pain and attempted to awaken my mother who had only laid down to rest after being up for nearly 24 hours. My mother is often times the one who is the person you call to help when you are in a crisis, looked at me and asked what you want me to do. I asked her to call my doctor or an EMT for an ambulance.

Once she left the room and I was laying on her bed I made one huge push and the intense pain I had been feeling completely stopped. I was unaware of exactly what had happened. I was just happy the pain stopped. Shortly after this occurred, 2 different groups of EMT professionals entered the room. They pulled my son out and began to check him and get him to cry. In the first ambulance was my son being taken to the hospital in the next county and I followed behind him in another.

Upon returning to the same hospital I initially visited the night before when my contractions were so intense. I requested that the chaplain be sent to my room. Once the chaplain entered the room, I explained that my baby would not make it and it was my desire to have him dedicated to God. He held my son in his arms, asked his name, prayed over him, christened him, and returned him back into my arms. I spent the next few moments talking to my son, James. My doctor made it into the room at this time and for the first time during my pregnancy appeared to be sad. He explained that my amniotic sack had not dislodged, and he would have to remove it.

After this procedure was done, my family and friends began to flood the room. I was holding my son when his father and aunt arrived at the hospital. As soon as his father entered the room and picked him up, his name went from James to Jamie and for the first time our son opened his eyes and smiled at us. The next few hours Jamie rested in love in his father's arms or in mine. Hours had passed and I looked at Jamie's dad's eyes and knew that our son had transitioned. It was not until much later that Jamie's dad told me that he had gone long before he let me know, but he was not ready to release our son.

After all our family and friends left, Jamie's father and I spent the night in the hospital. I asked the nurse for our son as I knew soon, he would have an autopsy and we would have to relinquish him to the funeral home. For the next hour I spent holding Jamie, talking to his father, and pointing out just how much he looked like him. After my release from the hospital, the day was spent making funeral arrangements and trying not to get lost in my grief.

Looking back, how I got through this extremely painful period in my life was through the grace of God, my parents being there, and I had frequent conversations with Jamie's father. There were nights I stayed with him to sleep, being near him brought me peace, and he seemed to be the only one that knew exactly how I felt. On my road to healing there were many ups and downs. I made the decision to help children around me that were hurting and in doing so it began to heal my heart.

CHAPTER 2
THE FIGHT OF MY LIFE

By: Perita H. Adams

"As Jesus went with him, he was surrounded by the crowds, A women in the crowd had suffered for twelve years with constant bleeding, and she could find no cure. Coming up behind Jesus, she touched the fringe, of his robe Immediately the bleeding stopped." –Luke 8:43

BASIC TRAINING

I decided to start my story on this Christmas Eve of 2019. The reason for this decision is because this is the first realization that I have to proclaim I'm a survivor, an overcomer, and a winner. When I agreed to collaborate in this series, "Down for the Count," I thought wow, I've been through a lot in my life just as many of you have! So, how do I drive it home about this battle I endured that practically knocked me senseless?

At the age of nine, I remember suffering the most excruciating pain possible. This pain seemed to be a result of my menstrual cycle. At that time, I didn't fully understand what was going on with my body except what I was told; that young girls around my age experienced a change that meant we were growing into young ladies.

I would like to stop there for just a moment to discuss how mothers and daughters should discuss what to expect when they become of age. Our body changes and so do our emotions. This phase in life is sensitive and important however, if properly prepared for can make a major difference in handling physical alerts.

As I mentioned being only nine years old, I thought maybe since this is my first month, the pain may be a little more uncomfortable. Boy was I wrong!! What would occur over the next several years would be more than a fight. It would be a battle!

For most of my pre-teen years, I suffered. Every month my body braced for a fight which consisted of pain on a scale of 1-10, it was an eleven!!! My menstrual cycle lasted for a nightmare of three to five days and I couldn't eat or think clearly. My body would be folded into a fetal position either on the bed, floor, or in the bathroom as I cried in severe pain and practically blacked out. I felt like someone literally gut-punched me.

HUNGRY BUT NOT ABLE TO EAT!!

My body would be lethargic from weakness because I couldn't eat. If I tried to eat, I would vomit uncontrollably. It was as if my digestive system had failed. My body couldn't digest and process my food.

I couldn't go to the bathroom to relieve myself because my bowel and uterus had literally grown together, as a result of scar tissue from the endometrial lining in my uterus. So my body developed its own unique way to keep me alive by excessively vomiting. Since I hadn't yet been properly diagnosed, I didn't know the extent of what type of fight I was truly in. The fight for my very life!

SURVIVAL – I WILL LIVE

I learned to eat just enough food to keep me from being weak. Although I still threw up, because I didn't eat much, my digestive system didn't have to work hard, so the pain was a little more controllable. Heat was my friend. I learned that sitting in a bathtub of extremely hot water gave me comfort and felt tolerable. Therefore, I would sit in the bathtub for 2-3 hours replenishing the hot water as the water grew cold. I would stay in the bathtub so long I would practically fall asleep.

Finally, I felt like externally I was learning to cope. Now I must soothe the internal pain so I learned to take Pepto-Bismol, which would ease my stomach discomfort and Pamprin, a medication for pre-menstrual pain wouldn't touch the pain. The pain didn't get any better so I decided to take Advil. During this time, I would stay out of public view as much as possible because the pain crippled me, and I felt vulnerable. For those who know me know that I'm a long way from that. I never go into a fight I can't win!! So, I learned to cope. My social calendar took a hit because I had no one that I knew who could identify with this opponent, let alone help me strategically train to beat it. But God!!!!! You see at a young age I knew God and had developed a relationship with him, and he gave me and you this special verse:

"Fear not, for I am with you; be not dismayed, for I am your God; I will strengthen you, I will help you, I will uphold you with my righteous right hand. Behold, all who are incensed against you shall be put to shame and confounded; those who strive against you shall be as nothing and shall perish. You shall seek those who contend with you, but you shall not find them; those who war against

you shall be as nothing at all. For I, the Lord your God, hold your right hand; it is I who say to you, "Fear not, I am the one who helps you." –Isaiah 41:10-13

I spoke it every day, I lived it every day, and I kept my boxing gloves on!!

ROUND 1

Knowledge is Power- In order to win this fight. I must know what I was up against. I knew this because God said, *"Therefore my people are gone into captivity, because [they have] no knowledge: and their honourable men [are] famished, and their multitude dried up with thirst." Isaiah 5:13*

Therefore, I had to know. In life, we wrestle against principalities not knowing the underlying cause, so in order for us to win we must give it a face even if it seems faceless. Then we can land the punches we need to win!!

For most of my younger years, the doctors would say to my mother: she's just having severe menstrual cycles, put her on birth control pills and that should diminish it. Wrong!!! As I continued to fight year after year, and round after round, I decided by my eighteenth birthday that I would save my own money and seek out the advice of a specialist.

It was official! My eighteenth birthday came and that very next week I had my appointment. I thought once the doctor discovered what was wrong with me, I would have my diagnosis, he could treat me, and I would be able to move on from this fight. Yay!! I made it!

Well, the news came in. You have Endometriosis. Okayyyyyy!

Now what? Well, as the doctor explained, you have a lot of scar tissue which is causing your severe pain. That's the good news. Huh! The bad news is that the only way to fight it is surgery which could cause more scar tissue. A hysterectomy (there goes my chance at motherhood)? Or medication to stop my cycle, which will give me a chance to get pregnant.

Hello, I'm only 18!! I was tired, scared, and angry but no way ready to give up the fight. So, I picked up my boxing gloves on the way back out the door of the doctor's office along with brochures, pamphlets, my x-rays, and diagnosis. I didn't win this round but my opponent finally had a face and history. Now I could see where his strengths and weaknesses were and prepare for my next round.

PREPARATION

I was always a critical thinker. How could I handle this issue and be as normal as possible? In a fight, the fighter must not only be physically fit, but one must be equally, mentally and strategically prepared. As God says, my people perish for lack of knowledge. I became strategic. When you fight an opponent, you must do your homework. So, I did an S.W.O.T. Analysis.

- What was my opponent's strength? The ability to give me extreme cramps, severe pain, nausea, and weakness. My strength was Advil, hot water (water bottle), prior rest, research and mind over matter.
- What was my opponent's weakness? It only came around once a month during my menstrual cycle and lasted 3-5 days. My weakness would be not to be prepared for the inevitable.

- Opportunity- this Endometriosis could kill me but only if I let it!!
- Threat-my very livelihood was being taken away from me. The ability to have a family, children and a normal life.

SO LET THE FIGHT BEGIN!

ROUND TWO

As God as my coach, I constantly read my word and prayed. This was big! How could little 18-year-old me win. Then I read this verse.

> *"Finally, be strong in the LORD and in his mighty power. 11 Put on the full armor of God, so that you can take your stand against the devil's schemes. 12 For our struggle is not against flesh and blood, but against the rulers, against the authorities, against the powers of this dark world and against the spiritual forces of evil in the heavenly realms. 13 Therefore put on the full armor of God, so that when the day of evil comes, you may be able to stand your ground, and after you have done everything, to stand. 14 Stand firm then, with the belt of truth buckled around your waist, with the breastplate of righteousness in place, 15 and with your feet fitted with the readiness that comes from the gospel of peace. 16 In addition to all this, take up the shield of faith, with which you can extinguish all the flaming arrows of the evil one. 17 Take the helmet of salvation and the sword of the Spirit, which is the word of God. 18 And pray in the Spirit on all oc-*

casions with all kinds of prayers and requests. With this in mind, be alert and always keep on praying for all the LORD's people." –Ephesians 6:10-18

So, I'd like to say the fight was quick, but it took many more rounds before I could see my victory, but it doesn't mean that you are losing. It just means that you are getting stronger. I had surgery after surgery. I was picked and probed. Doctor after doctor. I stayed in the fight. The library was my best friend, but the word was my Physician's Manual, Inspiration, and Boxing record.

THE KNOCK- OUT PUNCH

I moved on with my life. At 21 years old I met and married the man of my dreams. He was kind and understanding. He knew that the possibility of me having children was next to none. All he wanted was me. God showed up four years later and blessed me with a beautiful baby boy named "Tony." Sometimes we get so hooked up on fighting the battle that we forget we've already won. Lastly, God gave me this scripture:

"He said: "Listen, King Jehoshaphat and all who live in Judah and Jerusalem! This is what the LORD says to you: 'Do not be afraid or discouraged because of this vast army. For the battle is not yours, but God's." –2 Chronicles 20:15

Ironically, I had been fighting a battle that wasn't even mine. You see for many years I was that lady with the issue of blood. But God, gave me a transfusion and cleansed me. Many of you know what I'm talking about. When it seems the very life has been knocked out of you, I got news for you. **KEEP FIGHTING!!!**

I've been that man on the mat trying to get to the water to be cleansed and healed. It was only when I picked up my own mat and carried it that I was redeemed. Pick up your mat so you can win!!

It was many years later, after I truly gave it to God, I had a hysterectomy and the bleeding and pain stopped. I stepped over my opponent Endometriosis and recited this verse:

" For whatsoever is born of God overcometh the world: and this is the victory that overcometh the world, our faith." –1 John 5:4

My trust and faith in God delivered the final punch of my victory. Now lift up your prayer and praise.

BECAUSE YOU ARE A WINNER!!!

Chapter 3

Finding Purpose through the Pain!

By: Stephanie V. Barnes

"Many are the plans in the mind of a man, but it is the purpose of the LORD that will stand." –Proverbs 19:21

How did I get here? I thought I was just investing into my dream. In November 2012, just days after my 40th birthday, I became anxious about what I thought had not taken place in my life. I desired something different in the realm of relationships and sought it out in the wrong place. This emotional encounter changed the course of my life. It started by sharing a dream of being financially independent with an individual I met through a Christian social media platform. He had extensive business knowledge and excellent communication skills. He listened very carefully to my words and created a perfect picture.

I was excited about the opportunity of becoming an entrepreneur and having someone to walk with me on the journey. Little did I know, the willingness came as a result of a well-developed scheme implemented before it all began. The air was quickly filled with promises I shared with family and friends. Yet, the commitments were warning signs, which led to moments of low self-esteem, depression and extreme debt. The adventure had been skillfully crafted for anyone who travelled down the "runway of opportunity." It was a calculated plot to get rich through the sacrifice of others.

In my moment of desperation to fulfill my desire, I had faced my greatest fear. I walked into a trap that had been deployed for some time and had been successful at capturing others. By the time I realized what had happened, it was too late. In a matter of months, I had invested everything; self, time and money in exchange for gifts and false promises about the future. The dream of owning a transportation business had materialized, however, I faced tremendous pain along the way. I was only a valuable player for the financial operations, with no regard for my well-being. Every decision I presented for the business was criticized as well as my personality and character. I wanted the business practice to be established on the principles of accountability, integrity and excellence. It became the exact opposite.

It appeared I had lost control of my life. Greed, manipulation and deception sought me out and won temporarily. I thought I was dreaming but quickly realized it was **REAL** and the pain was real! Daily, I was bearing the agony of living with the mental and financial distress caused by trusting someone else's plan. I felt as if I had been dropped off in the war zone and met the enemy. My pride had given an indication that I was equipped for the fight, considering I had years of military training, but I needed more than that.

I wanted to give up. Instead, I had to rely on what I knew best—faith, family and friends. Initially, I was afraid to talk about it because of pride and shame. I could not believe I had allowed this to happen to me.

With limited funds and tons of overdue lender notices, I had to return to my hometown and live with my family. My vision was clouded with thoughts of the events and I just could not see. My mother advised me to speak with my spiritual father who coached me through the deliverance process. I had to be delivered from myself. I had to forgive and learn to love everything about myself. I was on my back crawling through life but determined to get back up and walk again. Then one day, I woke up, cleaned myself up and continued on the journey. As the days passed, I regained the courage, wisdom, and strength I needed to keep moving forward. Most importantly, it fostered a stronger bond with my mother. We had a good relationship, however, after experiencing the greatest blow of my life, she and my sister were there to assist me in getting up. My mother taught me how to laugh again and not be so serious about matters.

The laughter and joy of finally realizing it was not my fault. It was like reliving my childhood with my adult siblings. I believe God sent me back home to get a few more life lessons!

That was it! I had to undergo the encounter. It propelled me to new spiritual heights and platforms. I had to be broken in order for God to prepare me for Kingdom work!

Professionally, I had mastered most things I wanted to do. It was my spiritual life that needed to be adjusted. First, I had to be healed from the pain. Forgiveness became my roadmap to healing! Then, I accepted my kingdom assignment and went to work. My mother would always tell me to be about the Father's business. Meaning, if I'm committed to working for God, He will provide all I need. I had to labor in the midst of the storm. *Jeremiah 29:11 states: "For I know the plans I have for you," declares the Lord, "plans to prosper you and not to harm you, plans to give you hope and a future."* God knew there was more inside of me. I had to be pruned in order to be prepared for a greater future. Returning home to my family and the ministry became the place of preparation for what God has given me over the past seven years. He orchestrated it all for His Glory!

Additionally, through this situation I discovered my purpose of being a respected speaker and teacher of leadership development. I love encouraging others and seeing them grow. Yes, it was a painful experience, but it helped me tap into some areas that had been dormant in my life. Today, I am grateful for the transformation that led to my purpose.

Some Lessons Learned (in no particular order)

- *Be Transparent*: First talk to God about how you are feeling. Ask Him to help with the pain and who you can trust with the sensitivity of the circumstances. Then talk it out until it becomes your testimony!
- *Forgive:* Seek spiritual guidance and begin to pray for the gift of forgiveness. It's important to forgive in order to move on. It will not happen overnight or within days, so do not become overwhelmed by the emotional part of this process.
- *Trust God:* Do not be distracted by what you lost. Assess the situation and release it unto God. He will see you through and restore every aspect of your life.
- *Be willing to make the necessary adjustments:* This may require moving, changing your daily habits, checking your associations, connecting to support groups (based on the situation).
- *Ask for Help:* Rely on your trusted agents for support-family and friends from community, faith-based or other professional organizations.

- *Believe in Your Dream:* Do not allow someone to determine your dream. They can help cultivate it but not produce it. Follow your heart and listen to your inner soul. It will lead and guide you.
- *Acknowledge the Purpose:* Understand there is a Purpose in the Pain. You do not know what that will be until it is revealed/developed. You can count on experiencing growth through the pain/hardship!

PERSONAL NOTES

» Understand that when you hit rock bottom, there really is no place to go but up, if you believe, forgive and follow God's plan.

» Dream Big! Never attempt to live out someone else's dream (thanks Dad)!

» Time does HEAL the pain!

This chapter is designed to assist with whatever circumstances you have encountered or people you may need to forgive, including yourself. On the journey of forgiveness, I have met others who have experienced similar pain. I pray this will be encouraging and helpful to understand that we cannot alter a person's behavior or situation. However, you can become aware of who you are and how you respond to it. I'm a better person because of the process!

BE WELL!

Chapter 4
It Took a Miracle

By: Calotta Davis

"But He was wounded for our transgressions, He was bruised for iniquities; the chastisement for our peace was upon Him, by His stripes we are healed." –Isaiah 53:5

I can remember running and playing in the yard. I can hear my Mother calling me to dinner. My Father, Julius Mathews passed away November 1976. He had a stroke on the brain. So, I was expecting him to die. I had remembered my sister-in-law being killed in a car crash, so I knew how death hurt. My Mother took care of everyone and mailed packages to family members. She loved people. I turned sixteen years old in October 1977 and she died on Christmas Day. I woke up happy yet sad because my Mother was in the hospital. She called all ten of her children and then told me they were releasing her from the hospital. But before I left, she told me where to find money that she had pinned in the lining of a coat pushed in the back of a small closet.

I was so happy that she was coming home and didn't think anything about it. My Aunt had come to stay across from us, she was blind and wanted to ride with me. I remember stepping off the elevator and I could hear them calling a code blue to her room.

I was very curious, so I knew what that meant. Not good, I left my Aunt at the door of the elevator and ran down the hall. They grabbed me as I went in the door, she looked like she was asleep. Christmas Day, I didn't know what I was going to do. I was the baby of ten and now I felt a big knot, like someone had kicked me, and I was numb. Yes, my dear sweet Mother Georgia was gone.

I didn't take this tragedy so well. I had to grow up real fast. I stayed with my sister Gloria for about a year then my Sister Mattie's fiancé was walking to his car, had an aneurism and died. This was my ticket out of Eastaboga, Alabama.

After moving to Hartford, CT., I became very rebellious yet keeping my honor roll. I felt as though my Mother was looking down on me and I wanted to make her proud. I begin to play softball with the Hals Gals. I never learned Spanish, but my home room was A-Z Martinez. Go figure. So, I was very healthy. I graduated with honors from Hartford High School despite getting pregnant in my senior year. They created a program for me and by age 17, I had my own apartment. On March 26, 1980, I had my first child Othecka Mathews. Yes, she was born to Michael Jackson's music and I went right back in my clothes.

I met the love of my life Samuel Davis Jr. He was the son of a Bishop. I was brought up in church singing and leading songs at the age of six years old at Salem Baptist. I never thought I would marry a Pastor's son. But during my engagement, I was brutally raped. That's when I realized the power of God.

My husband has always been there for me. This was a very traumatic time for me, and I promised the Lord if he brought me through that situation, I would serve him until the day I die. So, we were married Oct 2,1982. Then I started to work in ministry, always singing but I walked around angry. Now as I look back, I needed God to Heal Me.

We have 3 children, Othecka Mathews, Katrina and Thomas Davis , eight grands and one great grandson that brings so much joy. I am their biggest cheerleader. I was working as a Medical Assistant and I found out I had bronchial asthma. So, I stayed sick in the cold winters. One day I came home with frozen tears on my face. My husband said we are moving you to a warmer climate. He took a fifty percent pay cut to move me back to Alabama so I wouldn't be so sick. *Love is what it does.* It was good and an honor to be home working with Bishop Edward and Mattie Thomas at Holy Hill Church of Our Lord Jesus. I found myself again directing the choir. After finding employment at Talladega College, I had an opportunity to work with my husband on campus. I began to have problems climbing the stairs though. What is this? "It's just my asthma flaring up," I told myself and that's what they treated me for. But it got worse instead of better. Eventually I had to leave my job.

We begin to commute to Douglasville, GA., to attend Victory Family Life Church. I began to work in the office as the Church Administrator. I found my passion working with the Youth. We had a step team, youth praise team, and a drama department. I begin to write and produce stage plays and it was amazing to see what I wrote, come to life. I was feeling as excited and motivated as I had ever been.

In 1998, I was ordained as a Minister and accepted my call as an Evangelist. Pastor Rogers and Pauline Murray were grooming us for our Now. Then the sickness came back with a vengeance. This made leading Praise and Worship very difficult. Eventually I had to stop singing and stop preaching. Finally, I got a diagnosis I had Sarcoidosis in both lungs, and they were black. They informed me there was no cure and told me to try to prepare for as much of a quality of life as I could. *Wow! I needed a miracle.*

I would not accept the report. Whose report will you believe?

I shall believe the report of the Lord. My husband said we are moving to North Carolina to work with a ministry. We moved and worked with Pastor Dexter and Tammy Perry at Greater New Life Ministry. I began to work in the Health Care Industry. After being a supervisor at Field Work Atlanta for thirteen years, it was very different. I began to move more into Outreach by teaching Bible Study at Kittrell Job Corp and assisting my husband with the Gospel Choir at Louisburg College.

I had a doctor's appointment and the doctor called me in the office. Oh no, this can't be good I thought. He had me to read my report out loud. No signs of Sarcoidosis! My miracle had come. I begin to say, thank you, Jesus, right in the office.

After my miracle, I returned doing Praise and Worship, and leading songs in the choir. The Lord blessed us after serving for twelve years, to start our own ministry. Pastor Samuel Davis, founded One Heart Ministry Inc., in May 2015, where every heart matters. I began Divine Women Heart to Heart Inc., in 2014 where my motto is, "Ministering to the Scars of a Woman."

After the miracle God has shown me, I didn't give up on the promise. In 2017, I released my first CD, *Destined for Greatness*. My scars don't define who I am. The rape didn't cripple me mentally to the point I couldn't teach safety to the young ladies. Down for the Count, Volume IV has blessed me to be able to share a chapter on my miracle.

I am now the founder and CEO of Spreading the Gospel Network where our ultimate goal is to spread the gospel all over the world; through our radio broadcast, TV broadcast, which airs on the Gospel America Channel. I wanted to push and promote the Kingdom of God and business through my monthly digital and print magazines and we are doing just that!

NEVER GIVE UP ON YOUR MIRACLE!

Chapter 5
I am an Overcomer

By: Stephanie Debnam

"And he said unto me, my grace is sufficient for thee: for my strength is made perfect in weakness. Most gladly therefore will I rather glory in my infirmities, that the power of Christ may rest upon me." –2 Corinthians 12:9

I was born August 17, 1978 and my life started off very interesting. When I was born, me and my mother almost died due to me being a premature baby and a twin. My twin sister, Barbara, was born breech and I was in my mother's rib cage. My mother had to give me blood and I stayed in the hospital until I was strong enough to come home. My twin sister, on the other hand, was born with no complications. But one night, 4 months later, when we were both asleep in the same crib, my aunt went to check on us and my twin sister was blue. She had died from S.I.D.S. This was the start of my story and a journey that only God could protect me from. Before my first birthday, my father was killed over an incident involving "change for a dollar" at a restaurant that he worked at...he was only 20 years old.

Fast forward to my teenage years and at the age of 14, I gave birth to my first-born son, Angelo Joseph Williams. I hid my pregnancy from my mother because I was out in the streets looking for love in all the wrong places. I had no father. My mother was hooked on drugs, so I turned to the streets. This is where I was able to get away from the hell I was going through at home. I was young, dumb and naive. I finally told my mother. I gave birth to a premature baby boy weighing only 3 lbs. and 3 oz. At this point, I knew that I didn't want my son to experience the life I had to live due to my mother's drug habit. But I was in for a big surprise when my son and I were in my mother's house, AJ was 1 years old at the time and I was feeling very ill like I had to use the bathroom. So as I sat on the toilet, I was in so much pain. I pushed very hard and I felt a pop.

I realized that I was in labor and a baby came out. I held him until my mother came back from the store. When she came in the house, I yelled for her to come to the bathroom and showed her my 2nd born son, Justin Jose Williams.

I couldn't understand. I was 16 years old with 2 children. I didn't even know that I was pregnant, so it was a shock to me and my family. At this point, my mother threw me and my kids out of her house and my friend's mother took me and my children into her home. She then told me that I had to get emancipated so that I may go into a homeless shelter in New York City. She took me and helped me through the process and then a judge granted me the emancipation because in the eye of the law I was an adult. I was able to get my own public assistance case and go into the shelter with a 1 year old and a premature baby. Justin was born when I was 5 months pregnant. He was a 1 pound baby born on the toilet.

I never thought twice about keeping my kids. I knew that I had to take care of them by any means necessary. Their fathers denied them from the moment I told them I was pregnant and had given birth.

I was all alone with 2 babies at the age of 16. I went into the shelter where I was stabbed 5 times in my back by a woman who was going through post-partum depression…this all happened in front of my kids. I had to sign myself out of the hospital and go back because I was determined to get permanent housing for me and my kids. I returned to the shelter. The next day I was transferred to a different location where I remained for the next 2 years until I finally was offered Section 8 and an apartment in the Bronx.

All along I was going to physical therapy with my youngest son, Justin so he could learn how to walk, due to him being born so premature. I was living in my apartment with my kids for about a year, when one day I asked my next-door neighbor to watch the boys while I went to do laundromat across the street from my building. She came over to the house to watch them for me. I came back after loading the clothes in the machine and I timed it so I could go back to put them on to dry. When it was time for me to go back, I told my neighbor she said okay. I went back to the laundromat and before I could finish loading the clothes, someone called me to come back upstairs because there was a social worker at my door and the kids were home alone.

I ran upstairs and when I got to my apartment, she said that AJ had opened the door for her and they were in the house all by themselves. I tried to explain to her that my neighbor was supposed to be watching them, but she said she was going to call child services on me. Well she did, and that evening as I was feeding the boys, I got a knock on the door. It was an investigator for child services. He came in the house and looked around. He asked me questions. He said everything is good, someone will come tomorrow to talk to me. Mind you, my house was always spotless. The boys had everything and more! I worked so hard to provide for them.

The next day as I waited for the worker to come talk to me and when she arrived, she came with the police and they took my kids from me. I lost my mind. I didn't know what to do. I went to court. I fought for them and my sister even tried to get custody of them, but she was denied. The woman that had them was a known foster parent and she wanted to keep my boys and adopt them. As I went back and forth to court and fought for my boys, they made me out to be the worst mother in the world. They said that my kids were better off with her. This happened because I was young, I didn't have any support system and the social worker had it out for me. The last thing the judge said to me was that my rights were taken and from that moment on, I was dead to my children.

After I picked myself up off the floor, I had no one to turn to and my mother blamed me for years. Who I thought was my friend, introduced me to drugs to numb my pain and it went all downhill from there. I was drinking and using drugs for the next 12 years. I was a functioning addict that went to work every day, but it was only to feed my habit. One day I decided to confess to my sister who was saved and served the Lord. I told her that I was addicted to drugs and I needed help or I would die. She prayed with me and that day I gave my life to the Lord. I accepted Jesus Christ as my personal savior and from that moment on everything changed in my life.

I left New York City and moved to South Carolina, not even one week later my brother called me and said I think I found the kids on a social media platform called Myspace. I went on the site. It was them, my boys! This is 13 years later.

I sent AJ a message and told him that I was his mother and I left my phone number. Minutes later he called me and we spoke briefly. He cried so loud on the phone. We both cried. It was my dream come true! I reunited with both of my boys and today I have a grandson, Aiden, 2 years old and just to hear them call me Mom keeps me alive.

I have been serving God with all my heart. I recently got married one year ago. My husband is a God-fearing man. I have an amazing support system and church family. My sister passed away on 12/16/18, and the one thing she left me was the Word of God. She was obedient to the Lord and planted that seed that continues to grow in me every day of my life. If it wasn't for God's Grace, Mercy and Love, I don't know where I would be right now, but he kept me all those years that I wanted to die. I had nothing to live for, so I thought, but his plans for me are greater than anything I could ever imagine.

Chapter 6
My Story but God's Glory!

By: Clara Darden Pitt

"I shall not die, but live, and declare the works of the LORD" –Psalm 118:17

Living in this life is just like a marriage -for better, for worse, for richer, for poorer, in sickness and in health, to love, cherish, and obey, till death do us part, according to God's holy law. Life and I are united together to conquer the world or to be defeated by the world. This union is challenging, but inevitable when going through the progression of living and dying.

According to the Merriam-Webster Dictionary, living means having life or being alive and dying means gradually ceasing to be or approaching death. As a believer of God's Holy Word, you will live a fruitful life as long as you are connected to the true living vine, my Lord and Savior, Jesus Christ. I am living to live again, but what do you do when life starts throwing you foul balls, curve balls, fast balls and even strikes. Balls were coming in a position that I was unable to hit; balls were coming filled with things that I was not expecting; balls were coming with such force that I could not react in time to even think about attempting to hit. Life began throwing balls that were coming as expected and with normalcy, but as I swung, I still missed.

Wow! What do you do when life throws you stuff that you cannot hit nor throw back? I had two questions for life:

1. **Did I have more love for you than you had for me?**

   or

2. **Did I have too many complaints about you?**

When I united with life, I was not given an option to divorce it. There would be no separation until death us do part. I had been linked to life for a long time and now it was on a mission to test me. The beginning of our relationship was calm, but now life was bringing me chaos and confusion. I did not know if life was trying to make me or break me. Will I be better off living with life or dying without it? I made a quick decision; I begged and pleaded with life to stay with me. In my mind I said, "Life I am sorry, I need you and I promise to be committed only to you; forget about the fun, the complaints, the neglects and the regrets. I will live with you and all your pitched balls."

In May 2001, the balls started coming when my dear friend, my mentor, my motivator, my mom was diagnosed with colon cancer. My mom was a virtuous woman , just as the ***Proverbs 31:20 woman, "she opened her hand to the poor and reached out her hands to the needy."***

My mom was a godly woman of strength that inspired her children and others how to live through loss and how to survive after suffering. After my mom's colon was removed, she was administered several chemotherapy treatments and took cancer pills. I watched as she lived a life filled with love, laughter, depression, anxiety, disappointment, faith, patience and peace. She never gave up, but life gave in. She grew weaker as the treatments increased and the cancer continued to spread.

On January 12, 2002, my mom's earthly life ended. At that time, I was still a babe in Christ, but I had developed a relationship with God, and I knew that my mom would live again. God's holy word says, *"That whosoever believeth in Him should not perish, but have eternal life" John 3:15.* She was a believer and went on to live a real life in eternity with the Lord.

Why did life throw me this unwanted ball? I had just lost my best friend, my mom; and my heart was broken. I was furious with life and I wanted to say what I was feeling, but God reminded me that *"life and death are in the power of the tongue, and they that love it eat the fruit thereof" Proverbs 18:21.*

"Say what you mean and mean what you say," but whether it be good or evil you will acquire the consequences of your words. So, I made a declaration to God and another promise to life that cancer will not take me out. Cancer would not be my death sentence, but my chance to live in abundance. Life and I were still connected. I could not run away from it, but I needed help to keep running with it.

At this point, I began to get deeper into God's holy word and I needed answers. I needed understanding and peace of mind to be free from my negative thoughts of life. So, I began to ask God to show me His glory and to reveal to me how it is possible to progress with life and not digress from the journey. Lord God, show me, show me Your glory! Just as the Lord told Moses on his journey to lead the Israelites out of Egypt, out of captivity: *"The Lord replied, 'My Presence will go with you, and I will give you rest'" Exodus 33:14.* The Lord captured me in my spirit, and I changed my mind regarding life. As I matured in the Lord, life continued to throw me unwelcomed balls and I gained the strength and courage to grab a bat. I joined the MIT (Ministers in Training) at church, meditated on God's holy word more intimately and made an unexpected exit from the class. But God never started anything and left it unfinished. God led me back to the MIT class and He directed me to preach my initial sermon on March 26, 2006. God had called me; He had exalted me. God had lifted me up and my assignment was complete. This assignment was only the beginning of a greater plan and purpose that God had for me. Life and I were meeting in the middle, but there was still something missing in our relationship. I battled with life instead of battling against it. I attempted to swing at every ball that came my way. I hit some, missed some and some balls even knocked me down.

The battles started all over again. I had underestimated life, and it got more challenging than I ever imagined. I thought I was growing with it, but instead I felt as though I was dying in it. I thought that my mind had been renewed until the devil started attacking my body. I had one surgery after another: minor surgeries, major surgeries, office procedures, outpatient and inpatient. Life was throwing balls from every direction and I was getting exhausted. People did not have to know what I was going through unless I told them, but I needed to know. I asked God to reveal to me what I was doing wrong and what He wanted me to do right in order to get the bond of "holy matrimony" sealed between life and me. I petitioned the Lord God again to show me His glory! I tried to keep my feelings toward life on the inside, but life decided to make a grand appearance on the outside.

God placed me on a platform and spoke a word to my spirit. God said, "Not only will I show My glory to you, but others will see My glory in you and through you." "Be careful what you ask for." Life had thrown me many balls, but this one was unbelievable and inconceivable.

On June 17, 2012, I went to an emergency health facility with an excruciating pain in my upper left side. I was diagnosed with shingles based on my age and the position of the pain. The pain continued as I followed up with my primary physician the next week. After several tests, x-rays, bloodwork and lab results, the doctor called me after office hours to inform me that my sixth lateral rib was broken. I also was directed to a specialist, because some abnormalities had appeared in the bloodwork.

Again, after more tests, x-rays and bloodwork, I received a phone call from the specialist with a need to schedule my next appointment. I started to experience some anxiety as the call did not come from the nurse assistant nor appointment coordinator. The specialist also requested the presence of my husband to discuss the test results.

On August 16, 2012, the doctor, who greeted me with a hug, revealed to me with my husband by my side, in a calm still voice that I had cancer. I had been diagnosed with a disease that was listed as the cause of death on my mom's death certificate. Had life thrown me the final ball? Had I been destined to be separated from life by cancer? Had life decided to let me go or do I fight to keep it?

CHAPTER 7

THE WEAPON WAS FORMED, BUT IT DIDN'T PROSPER

By: Antionette Bey

"No weapon formed against you shall prosper...." -Isaiah 54:17a

At some point in my life, I came to the realization that I was placed on this earth for a divine purpose, but I wasn't sure what that purpose was. I never really gave it much thought even though I sometimes hoped that it would be revealed to me prior to this life being over. As a young adult, I believed my purpose was to be the primary caregiver to my ill mother. You see, when I was a young kid, I watched my mother attempt suicide. I was around seven or eight years old when my mother came and handed me an index card with my grandmother's phone number and stepdad's work phone number on it. She told me if anything happened to her to call my grandmother or my dad. There were things I knew about my mother's health that I didn't understand at the time but now looking back, I realize that everything was purposed for God to use it for His glory. A short while later, she took a handful of pills.

My mother was diagnosed with manic depression and because of all the medications she took, it was imperative that this little

41

mother hen knew every pill by name, its purpose, and when they should be taken so I knew undoubtedly that it was not medication time yet. As I watched several pills hit the floor and I stooped down picking them up asking, "Mommy why are you taking your medicine again and it's not time?" An ounce of anger and rage went through me because I questioned how an adult could be so stupid to take their medication outside the time listed on each bottle. I picked up the pills and put them back into their bottles as she went into the living room and lay down on the floor to drift off into her peaceful death.

Unlike most little girls, I spent the better part of my day sitting beside my mother reading a book, coloring, crocheting, or watching Sesame Street while she dozed in and out of sleep. During the summer months, I mostly sat outside our front door and periodically went inside to check on her safety. "Mama, I need you to lay on the couch and go to sleep," would be my directive if I wanted to play rope outside with what few friends I had.

By middle school, my mother was somewhat more emotionally healthy, but due to my traumatic experience, I was always afraid to leave her for too long. Therefore, I did not experience the most fulfilling childhood. All the while I wore an infectious smile. I was given the name "Smiley" by an elderly lady I once met. At that time, I thought my purpose was to make others smile although that didn't make since because I wasn't a funny person. I only had a smile that I wore with such posture to hide the real unrest that I felt as a little girl who lacked having a mother that was lively and vibrant like so many other mothers I'd seen.

This was a huge embarrassment to feel this way and even the truth of the matter was suppressed out of the guilt that, at least my mother didn't die that day and was still alive. What a burden for a little girl to have to carry alone. Satan knew exactly what tools to use in my life to attempt to destroy me. Loneliness, rejection, and fear can tear through the core of an individual leaving them heartless, hopeless, and distant from reality. You see, during this time in my life, I also experienced being sexually molested by a close friend of the family. At least that is as much as my mind has been able to conceive. God has allowed me to see glimpses of occasions where I was being violated as a little girl and in looking back, I can see how God allowed those experiences to be hidden behind His love, and grace. Because He blocked those things from my memory, I quickly forgave those who transgressed against me. I know many times the results are much more detrimental as some people end up becoming addicts to drugs, alcohol, sex, over-eating or other addictions. Some suffer from mental health disorders because of sexual abuse. However, my truth was not so. My truth is that, despite my situation, God chose to keep me intact to utilize me as a spokeswoman for the power of his Love.

I kept things together and learned to not formulate close bonds with others for extended periods of time. There was always the preconceived notion that if my own mother would attempt to leave me, others would too. To avoid that pain of others leaving, I left first. Life was easy. Before your friends find other friends to play with or hang around, you find another friend first. I know it was a sick way of thinking now but back then, it seemed to make sense to me. It was my way of not getting hurt by other people's selfishness. See, I couldn't leave family, but I could leave friends. It's funny how as a kid the whole mentality of checking out of relationships carried on into my adulthood. It authored me into developing extremely unhealthy personal relationships, so much so to the point that when I wanted to have a long-term committed relationship, I was incapable of such because neither did I comprehend, nor was I taught what a committed relationship was. My only commitment was caring for my mentally ill mother because I loved her, and she was all I had. I knew that if I lost her, I had nothing else to live for.

When I became a parent myself, my mother was much better aside from a few minor health issues that required her to have temporary assistance every now and again. Therefore, I still could not disconnect from the caregiver role for as much as I wanted to. One failed and a failing marriage and six children later, I decided it was time to allow God to take over the course of this matter with my mother and her health issues. She was now having bad seizures and the doctors were not sure of the cause. I spent many nights in the ER and hospital, once again, sitting next to my mother while she slept, or climbing in the bed next to her so that I could catch a short snooze until the physicians came in for an update. No one else partaking in the journey that I had traveled so many years alone, this time, now leaving my children to do so.

Surely now you can see why I thought my only purpose in life was to care for my ill mother. Finally, my grandmother was willing to travel to doctor appointments, bring her home with her and prepare the meals and do the tending too. Finally, I could breathe. Not so!

Now I was embarking upon another journey of being a care-taker. This time to my now ex-husband. I won't go into that story. That's another book. However, I will say to anyone who knows us personally, God knows the whole truth and that is all that matters. Once again, I can unequivocally say that God's hand was over my life that kept my mind in perfect peace. Don't misunderstand, I am by no means saying that I never questioned God. I questioned His love for me and at times felt He cursed me for some unknown reason. I finally got to the point of just simply giving up on the fact that God even existed because after all, surely a loving God wouldn't curse a little girl with a mother who didn't want or love her and then double curse her adulthood with a husband she had to spend the rest of her life with that cared more for money and drugs then he did for her and the children.

SAY IT AIN'T SO! This could not be the lot God had in life for this little girl who dreamed of becoming an adult and working for the Peace Corp and finally be able to donate her own money to the Jerry Lewis Telethon. God placed in me a servant's heart and because Satan knew this, seeds were strategically planted to destroy that heart of servitude, so I started building walls to keep people out.

If there was no one there to serve, I could easily transition from the girl who wanted to serve in the Peace Corps to the girl who wanted nothing to do with people outside of her own terms. If satan isolates you from the things that matter in life, it makes his work of death and destruction over you that much easier. Because I wanted to make a difference, be an example, and prove a point, I endured the jolts, bolts, and whips of Satan's torment. But God, I was shrouded behind His love, grace, and protection.

I remember on my 40th Birthday having to fight past the lies of Satan telling that little girl inside of me that no one, not even my children, loved me enough to want me. Afterall, my two children from my first marriage left to live with their father in another state. My oldest child after returning home from Afghanistan decided to move to the same state, all stating they never wanted to return to our hometown again. Was it the weather, scenery, the opportunities, or was it me, their mother? Satan would have had me to believe it was me, and for a moment I believed him because for 11 years, I was told I thought I was better than everyone else because I avoided trying to "fit in" with others.

Eventually I started believing it. After regaining confidence in myself, I worked towards self-improvement because it empowered me to be a better me. I began to embrace spending time alone and developing my "Encouragement Factor." I discovered that when life is beating you down and you have no one in your corner to say keep going, you might have to encourage yourself.

Based on Merriam-Webster's Dictionary, encouragement is defined as the act of encouragement, the state of being encouraged, or something that encourages. When you look closely at these definitions, you'll see that you may have to play numerous roles in your own personal life. You may have to commit the act of encouraging, while playing the part of being encouraged, as well as recognize the things or people that bring you encouragement. We never get to a point of not needing encouragement. There will be times when people don't see the greatness in us. Therefore, it's necessary to perfect each of these roles in our lives. It does not matter what hinderances lie within the parameters of your life, destiny breakers do not carry weight unless you allow them to.

CHAPTER 8
HE TURNS MY TRAGEDY INTO TRIUMPH

By: Dr. Michelle Lucas

"But Jesus beheld them, and said unto them, with men this is impossible; but with God all things are possible."
–Matthew 19:26

My father died when I was four years old. I remember my mother crying about my father's car accident, to look back on that period of my life, I considered it a blur. My mother and grandfather decided that I would move from New York to Swann Station, North Carolina. It is wonderful when family steps in and aids in the time of need.

Upon arriving in Swann Station, I became a part of the village. There is an old saying that it takes a village to raise a child. I thank God for my village. I had caring Aunts, Uncles, and Cousins that made me a part of the village. Another focal point in my life was Love Grove A.M.E. Zion Church. It was a church that embraced me in love. From the time that I entered the church, it was a training ground that groomed me to succeed in life. I learned to sing, speak and lead. More importantly, I learned a love for the Lord. The most valuable lesson it gave me was a tool for survival. It was because of my relationship with God that I have an anchor that keeps me through my achievements and failures.

In America, there is a large percentage of homes that are run by single parents or grandparents. Some would consider this a disadvantage. But I believe that God puts us in situations to position us for greatness. It is up to the individual to choose the path that will lead them to succeed or fail. Life is a game of choices. When I accepted Christ in my life at the tender age of ten, I didn't know that he would guide me into all truth. Along my journey, I discovered that whether I strayed or stayed on the path to righteousness, he still had his hand had on me.

We have been taught by society that we are less than and because of our brown skin that we don't count. Whether you are black or a different race, don't let anyone tell you that you are inferior. Just because you see dolls or magazine covers that do not embrace your likeness does not mean you are not beautiful. Remember you are God's craftsmanship. **When God made you, He made the best.** You are a diamond. Don't let anyone tell you otherwise.

The first twelve years of my life, I spent without my mother. I formed my opinions of who I was, based on what was said about me. I allowed negative things into my spirit. The enemy wants us to become the opposite of what God's word says, then negative seeds can grow deep and come up like weeds.

When I think of my tragedies, I think of them now as a set up for my victories. For every one that told me that I was ugly, I never have anything or do nothing with my life, I sincerely say, "Thank You." Earning negative comments push me to be more and do more.

When I was asking God why bad things happen, I did not know that it was for my making, my development. Every episode in life is not God cursing you or because something is wrong with you. When Jesus died on the cross, He won the battle for us. He won the court case. I declare myself a winner.

My heartaches and setbacks empowered me because of the love of Jesus Christ. I studied his word and learned that I could be better and do better. I did not have to remain in a place of lowliness. I'm learning that I have the victory in all things. I am discovering that despite what is happening, God loves me. I am standing still, putting my trust in Him, and things will work out. I believe things will work out.

When I look at the fact that I was raised with many disadvantages like my race, and at times, not have a strong support system. Once again, I have to say thank you, Jesus, I made it. As a Pastor and Professor, I now see myself in others. For example, when applying for a job, the request is usually for previous experience. I can now say whether I like it or not, I now have experience. It is a blessing to a mid-wife and to help give birth to other dreams.

I consider myself a fighter. Like a prizefighter, through Christ, I fight to win. There is something inside of me (the spirit of God) that keeps fighting. I believe that what has gone wrong in my life can be made right when I read my word and ask God to intervene.

There are seasons in our life that we have done what we wanted to do, made a bad decision and gotten ourselves in deep trouble. We must remember that there are some things that we get ourselves into that only God can get us out of, it is because of his grace and mercy that we are recused from our foolishness. What is so awesome about the Lord is that He allows us to make choices and He watches out for us when we make bad selections. It makes us aware of what went wrong and allows us to get it right with Him. When we fall with the Lord's help, we can get back up and walk.

The Bible speaks very highly of faith. When we go through a trial or test, it is designed to enlighten us that we may turn from a damaging mindset and to do some things in a more positive light. There are issues in life that we would never pursue if our trails or tests were not passed. I believe there are some things that we bring on ourselves; then, there are events that we are pushed to survive through that teach us a lesson.

All my life I always said that I did not want to go through anything. I did not understand why I had bad experiences. Now, I understand that they were for my making. It was also for those people that are going through the same thing that I experienced. When I witness to them, I could understand their pain. When you experience pain and hurt, you never forget, and it gives you a passion for bringing others out.

One thing that has kept me through my trials and helped me to overcome is my prayer life. It has allowed me to humble myself and be truthful and honest with the Lord. I can go before the one that I trust and bare my soul. I can say that Jesus is a friend that does not disappoint and always comes through. When I strive to do what is right, I reap positive results. The word tells us that if we seek Him, we will find Him. I want to know more so I continue to seek Him. My test is my testimony. I have experienced a lot of hurt and pain. For every trial, the Lord has given me the desires of my heart. When we hold on to his hand and stay in relationship, we will see results.

For me, my life has been a journey of setbacks and comebacks. I always had things that I had to bounce back from. I remember in the sixth grade, and I was told that I had scoliosis, a curved spine. I had to wear a brace for three years and it was hard going to school every day knowing that you had limitations. I realize now that when God is doing something special in your life, you may be the subject of ridicule, but in the end, He is going to allow you to shine brightly for Him.

The Father needs people that don't mind being mocked and have suffered. He wants those people who can say I may have been **DOWN FOR THE COUNT**, but you brought me out. If anyone can testify, that would be me. Jesus is my special friend. He is one I can depend on like no other. If only people would try him and find out how great he is. To know Him is to love him.

When I accepted Christ in my life as an adult (I received Christ in my heart in the 5th grade.) I have not looked back. I visualized the Lord taking my hand and never letting go. Even when I wanted to let go, he never let go. He has served in roles where there was a vacant area in my life. He was there when I felt I was all alone. He was my guide and best friend — what a great God. I have learned to breathe through my trials because I know that in the end, I will be triumphant.

About The Authors

Felicia C. Lucas, compiler

Felicia Lucas is a #1 International Best-Selling Author and 4 Time Best Selling Author, Speaker, Coach and Book Publisher. Minister Felicia and her husband, Pastor Kelvin Lucas, co-founded *Take It By Force Ministries*, Inc. a non-profit youth and young adult 501©3 organization and *Dominion Tabernacle Church*. They were married in 1997 and have three children.

As a business woman on the move, she is the CEO of *His Glory Creations Publishing, LLC* and the Co-Founder of *His Glory Creations Christian Store*, an online Christian and Inspirational Store.

She is the 2016 Recipient of the North Carolina Career Woman of the Year Award by the North Carolina Business and Professional Women's Club.

Felicia graduated from the University of North Carolina at Chapel Hill with a Bachelor of Arts Degree in Speech Communication. For over twenty years, she has worked in the human resources field.

In 2019, she completed the Cornell University Women in Entrepreneurship Program.

www.felicialucas.com

www.hisglorycreations.com

www.takeitbyforce.net

Facebook: Author and Speaker Felicia Lucas

Facebook: His Glory Creations Publishing LLC

Facebook: Take it by Force Ministries, Inc.

Instagram: Coach Felicia Lucas

Twitter: Movetoyourbestu

Other literary works by Felicia C. Lucas:

- Make it Happen: Moving Towards Your Best U!
- Get in the Game: A Teen's Playbook for Winning the Game of Life
- The Bounce Back: Triumphant Stories of Resiliency and Perseverance
- Invitation to Intimacy
- Down for the Count: Bouncing Back from Life's Blows-Volumes I-III
- He Knows my Name: Inspirational Stories of God's Love for His Daughters-Volume I
- Affirmations that Remind Me (Marilyn Porter)
- 100 Inspiring Words (Marilyn Porter)
- ABC's of Authorship
- Entrepreneurial Elevation (Cheryl Wood)
- Stuff: A Collection of Middle Schools Thoughts-Volumes I and II

STEPHANIE DEBNAM

Stephanie Debnam is a wife and a mother of two adult men, she also has a 2-year-old grandson. She was baptized at Mason Temple Church of God in Christ 2012. She has dedicated her life to serving God since she rededicated herself in 2018. She has worked in customer service for over 20 years as she is always helping others. She earned her certified OSHA certificate in NYC along with her going back to school to earn her G.E.D. She has a passion for helping young girls and mothers who do not have any family or support at home. She is always looking for ways to give back to the community. In 2018, she teamed up with the local community center to support a back to school backpack drive where she donated and raised up to 100 backpacks and supplies for less fortunate children in Raleigh.

stephaniedebnam@yahoo.com
Phone: 984-364-1296

Dr. Michelle Lucas

Dr. Michelle Lucas was born in Queens, New York, and raise in Swann Station, North Carolina. Michelle is a certified Christian life coach. She received a Hamartian award from the Greater Greensboro/Reidsville Negro & Professional Women's club. She is a Distinguish Toastmaster (DTM). Michelle served on the Commission on the Status of Women and various city boards. Dr. Lucas holds a bachelor's in business administration with a minor in administrative services as well as master's degrees in Christian counseling and divinity. She earned her doctorate in the philosophy of the African American ministry. She is currently pursuing a doctorate in Leadership. Michelle has done further study at Duke University and United Theological Seminary. Dr. Lucas has worked in the administrative and utility field for over thirty years. She is also an adjunct professor. Dr. Lucas is the pastor of Total Wholeness Ministries, Inc. in Greensboro, NC. She has one son.

Contact Information:

Email-michellelucasspeaks@gmail.com
Facebook-https://www.facebook.com/michellelucas.speaks
Linkedin-
https://www.linkedin.com/in/dr-b-michelle-lucas-30bb025b/
Twitter- https://twitter.com/MichelleLspeaks

TANYA DUBOSE-SMITH

Tanya is a graduate of Johnson C. Smith University with a Bachelor of Arts in Psychology. She is passionate about others and has been of service to many children and their families. Tanya's passion is helping those on their path to become spiritually, financially, and emotionally whole. She is an independent business owner with businesses that focus on your physical and financial health. She is a published best-selling author and a dynamic inspirational speaker whose words touch the lives of others in profound ways. She has been acquainted with various challenges throughout her life. From these obstacles, Tanya was able to identify principles to navigate and overcome them. One of the major challenges Tanya faced early in life was having a blood vessel burst on her brain that from accounts of her doctor she was not supposed to survive. You can connect with Tanya @ tandee07@outlook.com

Stephanie V. Barnes

Stephanie V. Barnes is an inspirational speaker, teacher and trainer of faith- based leadership and personal development. She was reared in Sims (Wilson County), NC and currently resides in the Washington, DC area. Stephanie is an active member of both the military and ministry. She feels her greatest assignment is being a servant leader for the Kingdom! Stephanie received an undergraduate degree in Sociology from Fayetteville State University and a graduate degree in Public Administration from Troy University. She enjoys quiet time by the sea (meditation), listening to inspirational music (therapy) and watching movies (medicine for the soul). It's been her family, friends, life lessons, and personal relationship with God that has accelerated the desire to continue to "live on purpose" and help others cultivate their purpose through self-assessment and passion. Stephanie's recent teaching project had a focus on living "Beyond Your Limits" to fulfill God's plan and purpose. Email: steppingstones2911@gmail.com

Perita H. Adams

Perita H. Adams is a publisher, humanitarian, author and motivational speaker. Born and raised in Charlotte, North Carolina at an early age, her parents knew one of her gifts was writing. During her later years in elementary school, she discovered the gift of artistry. By the age of nine, she was on the school newspaper, and had received acknowledgements in creative writing and art. Perita holds an Associate Degree in International Business in which she had the opportunity to study abroad in China, Africa, and Canada. She also has a BA in Organizational Communication from Wingate University. She is the owner of GeneSIS Consulting and a Certified Christian Life Coach which she enjoys helping women utilize their gifts and talents to be their best self. She holds many events for women geared towards self-enrichment, empowerment and sisterhood. Perita is also the owner of Voices Publications, LLC a platform designed to inspire, educate and motivate. For additional information contact her at: voicesmagazinecharlotte@yahoo.com

ANTOINETTE J. BEY

Antoinette J. Bey is affectionately known to many as Mrs. Ann. She was born and raised in Benton Harbor, MI. with her mother and brother who is four years older than her. She holds a BS in Psychology from Liberty University where she majored in Addiction & Recovery and minored in Christian Counseling. She left working in the mental health field in early 2019 to pursue her purpose as an entrepreneur, author, & mentor. She also works from home as a Customer Support Specialist for Whirlpool Corporation. She is a mom of 9 (six birth children and three love children) and wife to an awesomely handsome and AHMAZING husband, Mr. Quentin Bey whom God hand crafted just for her. Mrs. Ann hopes that her story of bouncing back from the blows of Satan inspires you to believe that no weapon can harm you.

For more info regarding her mentorship you can email her at mrsannbey@gmail.com. You can also connect with her on Facebook @MrsAnnBey.

Calotta Davis

Evangelist Calotta Davis, the baby of ten, was born and raised in Eastaboga Alabama. By the age of sixteen she had lost both parents. Not allowing her adversity to change her goals, she moved to Hartford Ct. She met the love of her life Samuel Davis Jr.

They have three children, eight grands and one great grandson where she is their biggest cheerleader. After moving back to Alabama where she worked at Talladega College. They moved to Douglasville GA where she served in ministry for thirteen years. Ordained in 1998, she excepted her call as an Evangelist. As Youth Leader, she became known for over thirty stage plays. She worked hard in NC, Kittrell Job Corp and Louisburg College. In May 2019, she stepped out into full-time ministry. Their Ministry Office houses, One Heart Ministry Inc, Divine Women, and her most recent venture Spreading the Gospel Network.

Contact Calotta:
    Mailing Address: 904 Dorsey Ave , Henderson NC 27536
    Website: www.bit.ly/spreadthegospel

CLARA DARDEN PITT

Clara Darden Pitt grew up in Walstonburg, NC and currently resides in Greenville, NC. Clara is the daughter of Clarence Darden and the late Ella Mae Jackson Darden. She is the wife of an amazing man, Dennis Pitt. She is the mother of two sons, one living and one deceased, and one daughter, acquired through the marriage. She also has six energetic grandchildren. In 1984, Clara earned a Bachelor's degree in Computer Science from East Carolina University. Since 1998, she has been a devoted member of Salvation and Praise Full Gospel Ministries under the leadership of Apostle Ed Thomas Edwards and Lady Brenda Edwards. She is currently the Assistant Pastor of Salvation and Praise Morning Glory Church in Tarboro, NC, where she has served for the past nine years. Clara is a first-time author, and this is just the beginning. She looks forward to sharing the continuation of her life experiences and testimonies to encourage you never to give up on God.

Facebook: Clara Pitt

Email: pitthoney@gmail.com

Kelvin K. Lucas, Foreword Writer

Pastor Kelvin K. Lucas- husband, father, author and Leadership Coach whose journey towards servanthood began when he obtained his first job at the age of 16 at a local retail store. From that time, he began to embark upon learning a trade that has spanned for over 25 years and has taught him the essential key to empowerment...SERVING.

After attending North Carolina State University in Raleigh, North Carolina where he received a B.A. Degree in Business Management with a concentration in Marketing, Pastor Lucas took his trade to the next level by accepting a corporate executive position with a major retailer. Through those years he learned the leadership dimensions that would transition him into the next season of his life. He was ordained as an Elder in July 1999, and in 2001 co-founded Take it By Force Ministries, a 501© (3) organization that offers community outreach events, leadership, creative writing and life skills training for youth and young adults.

He and his wife, Felicia have been married since 1997, have three wonderful children, and are the Senior Leaders of Dominion Tabernacle in Rocky Mount, NC.

Contact Kelvin at:
Facebook: SimplyKelvin
Facebook: Take it By Force Ministries
Instagram: Simplykelvinlucas
Twitter: Simplyklucas
Website: www.simplykelvin.com

NOTES

NOTES

NOTES

NOTES

NOTES

NOTES

His Glory Creations Publishing, LLC is an International Christian Book Publishing Company, which helps launch and scale the creative works of new, aspiring and seasoned authors across the globe, through stories that are inspirational, empowering, life-changing or educational in nature, including poetry, fiction and non-fiction.

DESIRE TO KNOW MORE?

Contact Information:

CEO/Founder: Felicia C. Lucas

Website: www.hisglorycreationspublishing.com

Email: hgcpublishingllc@gmail.com

Phone: 919-679-1706